TAMPA BAY

BUCCANEERS

BY JOSH ANDERSON

Stride
An Imprint of The Child's World®
childsworld.com

The Child's World
childsworld.com

Published by The Child's World®
800-599-READ • www.childsworld.com

Photography Credits
Cover: © Mike Ehrmann / Staff/ Getty Images; page 1: © Africa Studio / Shutterstock; page 3: © Katharine Lotze / Staff / Getty Images; page 5: © Julio Aguilar / Stringer / Getty Images; page 6: © Rick Stewart / Stringer / Getty Images; page 9: © Brian Bahr / Staff / Getty Images; page 10: © Scott Halleran / Staff / Getty Images; page 11: © stevezmina1 / Getty Images; page 12: © Sarah Stier / Staff / Getty Images; page 12: © Bob Levey / Stringer / Getty Images; page 13: © Getty Images / Stringer / Getty Images; page 13: © J. Meric / Stringer / Getty Images; page 14: © Matthew Stockman / Staff / Getty Images; page 15: © Eliot J. Schechter / Stringer / Getty Images; page 16: © Brian Bahr / Staff / Getty Images; page 16: © Scott Halleran / Staff / Getty Images; page 17: © Al Messerschmidt / Staff / Getty Images; page 17: © Peter Read Miller / Associated Press; page 18: © Fma12 / Wikimedia; page 18: © Ezra Shaw / Staff / Getty Images; page 19: © Jamie Squire / Staff / Getty Images; page 19: © Sarah Stier / Staff / Getty Images; page 20: © Mike Ehrmann / Staff / Getty Images; page 20: © Chris Graythen / Staff / Getty Images; page 21: © Mike Ehrmann / Staff / Getty Images; page 21: © Kevin C. Cox / Staff / Getty Images; page 22: © Scott Halleran / Staff / Getty Images; page 23: © Brian Bahr / Staff / Getty Images; page 23: © stevezmina1 / Getty Images; page 25: © Patrick Smith / Staff / Getty Images; page 26: © Scott Halleran / Staff / Getty Images; page 29: © Al Messerschmidt / Stringer / Getty Images

ISBN Information
9781503857872 (Reinforced Library Binding)
9781503860674 (Portable Document Format)
9781503862036 (Online Multi-user eBook)
9781503863392 (Electronic Publication)

LCCN 2021952642

Printed in the United States of America

BRINGING THE WORLD TO YOUNG READERS 1968

TABLE OF CONTENTS

GO BUCCANEERS!

The Tampa Bay Buccaneers compete in the National Football **League's** (NFL's) National Football Conference (NFC). They play in the NFC South **division**, along with the Atlanta Falcons, Carolina Panthers, and New Orleans Saints. While the team has endured some long periods without making the **playoffs**, fans have also gotten to witness two **Super Bowl** victories by the "Bucs." And in 2020, the most successful player in NFL history took his talents to Tampa Bay. Let's learn more about the Buccaneers!

NFC SOUTH DIVISION

Atlanta Falcons

Carolina Panthers

New Orleans Saints

Tampa Bay Buccaneers

RUNNING BACK RONALD JONES II (RIGHT) RUSHED FOR 978 YARDS AND SEVEN TOUCHDOWNS IN 2020.

BECOMING THE BUCS

The Buccaneers joined the NFL as an **expansion team** before the 1976 season. The Seattle Seahawks began play during the same year. "Buccaneers" was chosen after fans submitted ideas in a name-the-team contest. During the 1600s, pirates were active in Florida's Gulf Coast. *Buccaneer* is another word for a *pirate*. The Bucs lost their first 26 games before finally winning the final two games of their second season.

HALL-OF-FAME QUARTERBACK STEVE YOUNG PLAYED TWO SEASONS WITH THE BUCS BEFORE HE BECAME A STAR WITH THE SAN FRANCISCO 49ERS.

BY THE NUMBERS

TWO
Super Bowl victories for the Bucs

511
points scored by the team in 2021—a Bucs record!

SEVEN
division titles for the Bucs

13
wins for the Bucs in 2021—most in team history!

THE BUCS HAD THE NFL'S THIRD-HIGHEST SCORING OFFENSE DURING THE 2019 AND 2020 SEASONS.

BUCS FANS CAN PAY EXTRA TO SIT IN THE PIRATE SHIP, WHICH WAS DESIGNED BY A PROP DESIGNER FROM DISNEY WORLD.

GAME DAY

The Bucs play in Tampa, Florida. Since 1998, they've played their home games in Raymond James **Stadium**. Before that, the team's home was Tampa Stadium. Fans have nicknamed the stadium "Ray Jay." It normally holds 65,618 fans, but it can expand to fit in about 10,000 more. Ray Jay has hosted the Super Bowl three times. One of the stadium's coolest features is a 103-foot (31-meter) pirate ship in the north end zone. The ship's cannons fire every time the Buccaneers score!

We're Famous!

When the most successful football player of all time comes to town, even the mayor notices! Quarterback Tom Brady won six Super Bowls as a New England Patriot before joining the Buccaneers. Before the team's matchup with the Kansas City Chiefs in Super Bowl 55, Tampa Mayor Jane Castor joked that if the team won, she'd rename the city "Tompa Bay."

UNIFORM

RED

WHITE

Truly Weird

During a 1983 game, Bucs coach John McKay decided he needed to make a change at kicker . . . during the game! After kicker Dave Warnke was far off on two attempts earlier in the game, McKay decided not to send him out again. Instead, he chose offensive lineman George Yarno to try an extra point. Amazingly, Yarno's kick made it through the uprights!

GEORGE YARNO

Alternate Jersey

Sometimes teams wear an alternate jersey that is different from their home and away jerseys. It might be a bright color or have a unique theme. In 2009, the Buccaneers wore their "Florida Orange" uniforms for the first time since 1996 and defeated the Green Bay Packers.

RAYMOND JAMES STADIUM IS A SEA OF PIRATE FLAGS ON GAME DAYS.

TEAM SPIRIT

Going to a game at Raymond James Stadium can be loads of fun! Several times throughout each game, the song "Yo Ho (A Pirate's Life for Me)" plays while prizes are thrown from the end zone pirate ship to nearby fans. The ship's permanent resident is Captain Fear, the team's pirate mascot. Captain Fear and the Tampa Bay Buccaneers Cheerleaders root on the team at every home game. And some hungry fans say they'd be willing to walk the plank to get hold of a Classic Cuban sandwich from Ray Jay's "Taste of Tampa" restaurants.

CAPTAIN FEAR

HEROES OF HISTORY

Mike Alstott

Fullback | 1996–2006

Alstott scored 71 **touchdowns** in his career—more than any other Buccaneer! He's the team's second leading rusher of all time, with 5,088 yards. A powerful fullback, Alstott was chosen for the **Pro Bowl** six times. He played a key role on the Bucs' championship team in 2002.

John Lynch

Safety | 1999–2003

Lynch spent more than a decade of his **Hall of Fame** career with the Bucs. The hard-hitting safety finished his career in Tampa Bay with 788 tackles and 23 interceptions. He was a key part of the team's defense during a time when it was among the best in the league.

Warren Sapp

Defensive Tackle | 1995–2003

Sapp played like an immovable mountain in the middle of the Bucs' defensive line during his nine seasons in Tampa Bay. A seven-time Pro Bowler, Sapp ranks second in team history with 77 **sacks**. He was elected into the Pro Football Hall of Fame in 2013.

Lee Roy Selmon

Defensive End | 1976–1984

The Buccaneers made Selmon the first draft pick in team history in 1976. Selmon is the franchise's all-time leader in sacks with 78.5 and forced fumbles with 28.5. In 1995, Selmon became the first Buccaneer inducted to the Pro Football Hall of Fame.

The Buccaneers defeat the Philadelphia Eagles in the team's first ever playoff game 24–17.

The Bucs win the Super Bowl for the first time. Behind five interceptions, they defeat the Oakland Raiders 48–21.

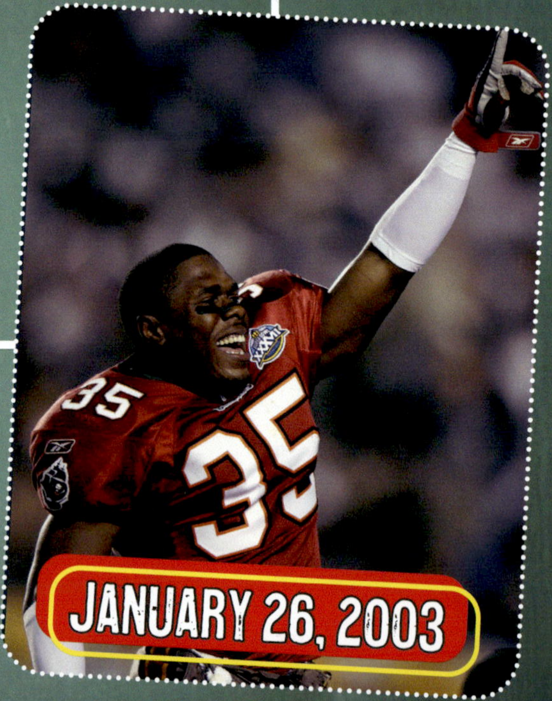

BIG DAYS

NOVEMBER 2, 2008

The Buccaneers come from 21 points down to defeat the Kansas City Chiefs 30–27. It's their greatest comeback ever!

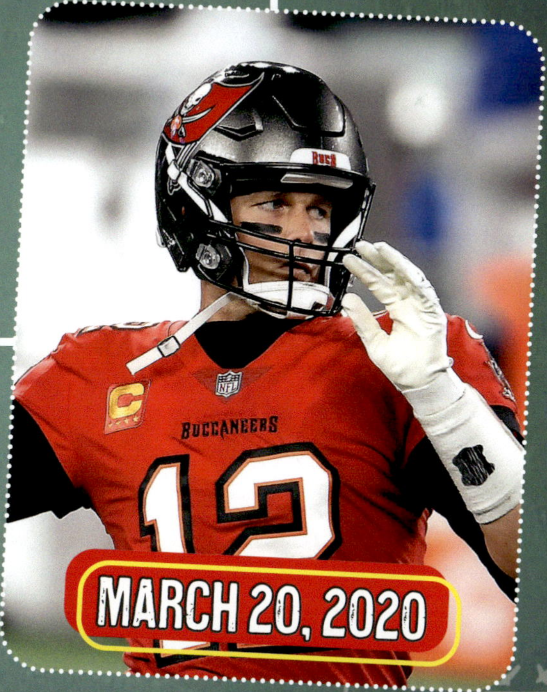
MARCH 20, 2020

The Buccaneers sign legendary quarterback Tom Brady to a two-year contract.

MODERN-DAY MARVELS

Tom Brady

Quarterback | Debut: 2020

A three-time **Most Valuable Player (MVP)**, Brady came to Tampa Bay hoping to bring the franchise its second Super Bowl victory. He passed for 40 touchdowns in 2020 and led the team to an 11–5 record. Then Brady helped deliver that championship in only his first year with the team.

Lavonte David

Linebacker | Debut: 2012

David was one of only two players in NFL history with 1,000 tackles, 20 sacks, and eight interceptions through their first eight seasons. In addition to anchoring the Bucs' linebacker unit, David has been a team captain since 2014. His 869 solo tackles rank third in team history.

Mike Evans

Wide Receiver | Debut: 2014

The Buccaneers selected Evans seventh overall in the 2014 NFL Draft. He is the only player in league history with more than 1,000 receiving yards in each of his first eight seasons. A four-time Pro Bowler, Evans was the leading receiver on the 2020 championship team.

Devin White

Linebacker | Debut: 2019

The fifth overall pick in the 2019 NFL Draft, White became an immediate star in Tampa Bay. He led the team with 140 tackles during the 2020 season. Then White had 38 tackles, two interceptions, and two fumble recoveries in the 2020 playoffs.

DERRICK BROOKS PLAYED EACH OF HIS 14 PRO SEASONS IN A BUCCANEERS UNIFORM.

THE GOAT

GREATEST OF ALL TIME

DERRICK BROOKS

Brooks ranks third in NFL history with 1,300 solo tackles. The 11-time Pro Bowler led Tampa Bay to its first Super Bowl victory after the 2002 season. His interception in the game's fourth quarter helped seal the Bucs' victory. Brooks was chosen for the NFL's All-Time 100 Team of the greatest players in league history. He was inducted to the Pro Football Hall of Fame in 2014.

FAN FAVORITE

#1

Dexter Jackson–Safety

1999–2002; 2004–2005

Jackson is beloved in Tampa for his heroics in Super Bowl 37. He intercepted Oakland Raiders quarterback Rich Gannon twice in the Bucs 48–21 victory. For his accomplishment, Jackson was named the game's MVP.

THE BIG GAME

FEBRUARY 7, 2021 – SUPER BOWL 55

The Buccaneers were underdogs coming into their Super Bowl matchup with the Kansas City Chiefs. Behind quarterback Patrick Mahomes, the Chiefs had one of the best offenses in the NFL. Tom Brady threw two touchdown passes to tight end Rob Gronkowski in the first half. The Bucs took a 21–6 lead into halftime. Running backs Leonard Fournette and Ronald Jones took over in the second half. All game long, the Bucs' defense was unstoppable. They held the Chiefs without a touchdown in Tampa Bay's 31–9 victory.

TOM BRADY PICKED APART THE CHIEFS' DEFENSE ON THE WAY TO THE SEVENTH SUPER BOWL VICTORY OF HIS CAREER.

TONY DUNGY LED THE BUCS TO THE PLAYOFFS IN FOUR OF HIS SIX SEASONS AS THE TEAM'S HEAD COACH.

AMAZING FEATS

1,454 Rushing Yards

In 2012 by
RUNNING BACK
Doug Martin

10 Interceptions

In 2001 by
CORNERBACK
Ronde Barber

15.5 Sacks

In 2002 by
DEFENSIVE END
Simeon Rice

20 Touchdown Passes

In 1980 by
QUARTERBACK
Doug Williams

ALL-TIME BEST

PASSING YARDS

Jameis Winston
19,737

Vinny Testaverde
14,820

Josh Freeman
13,534

RUSHING YARDS

James Wilder
5,957

Mike Alstott
5,088

Warrick Dunn
4,986

RECEIVING YARDS

Mike Evans
9,301*

Mark Carrier
5,018

Kevin House
4,928

SACKS**

Lee Roy Selmon
78.5

Warren Sapp
77

Simeon Rice
69.5

SCORING

Martín Gramática
592

Michael Husted
502

Connor Barth
477

INTERCEPTIONS

Ronde Barber
47

Donnie Abraham
31

Cedric Brown
29

*as of 2021
**unofficial before 1982

BUCS CORNERBACK RONDE BARBER PLAYED IN THE LEAGUE AT THE SAME TIME AS HIS IDENTICAL TWIN BROTHER, TIKI.

GLOSSARY

division (dih-VIZSH-un): a group of teams within the NFL who play each other more frequently and compete for the best record

expansion team (ek-SPAN-shun TEEM): a new team added to the league

Hall of Fame (HALL of FAYM): a museum in Canton, Ohio, that honors the best players in NFL history.

league (LEEG): an organization of sports teams that compete against each other

Most Valuable Player (MOHST VALL-yuh-bul PLAY-uhr): a yearly award given to the top player in the NFL

playoffs (PLAY-ahfs): a series of games after the regular season that decides which two teams play in the Super Bowl

Pro Bowl (PRO BOWL): the NFL's All-Star game where the best players in the league compete

sack (SAK): when a quarterback is tackled behind the line of scrimmage before he can throw the ball

stadium (STAY-dee-uhm): a building with a field and seats for fans where teams play

Super Bowl (SOO-puhr BOWL): the championship game of the NFL, played between the winners of the AFC and the NFC

touchdown (TUTCH-down): a play in which the ball is brought into the other team's end zone, resulting in six points

FIND OUT MORE

IN THE LIBRARY

Bulgar, Beth and Mark Bechtel. *My First Book of Football.* New York, NY: Time Inc. Books, 2015.

Jacobs, Greg. *The Everything Kids' Football Book, 7th Edition*. Avon, MA: Adams Media, 2021.

Sports Illustrated Kids. *The Greatest Football Teams of All Time*. New York, NY: Time Inc. Books, 2018.

Temple, Ramey. *Tampa Bay Buccaneers*. New York, NY: AV2, 2020.

ON THE WEB

Visit our website for links about the Tampa Bay Buccaneers:
childsworld.com/links

Note to parents, teachers, and librarians: We routinely verify our web links to make sure they are safe and active sites. Encourage your readers to check them out!

INDEX

ABOUT THE AUTHOR

Josh Anderson has published over 50 books for children and young adults. His two boys are the greatest joys in his life. Hobbies include coaching his sons in youth basketball, no-holds-barred games of Apples to Apples, and taking long family walks. His favorite NFL team is a secret he'll never share!